Amaranth

Amaranth

POEMS BY
LAURIE SHECK

The University of Georgia Press
Athens, Georgia

The publication of this book is supported by a grant from the National Endowment for the Arts, a federal agency.

Library of Congress Cataloging in Publication Data

Sheck, Laurie.
    Amaranth: poems.

    I. Title.
PS3569.H3917A8   811'.54   81-1934
ISBN 0-8203-0575-8   AACR2
ISBN 0-9203-0579-0 (pbk.)

Acknowledgments

The Antioch Review: "Brides"
The Ark River Review: "Two Children," "The Music of the Spheres,"
  "Letter from an Institution," "Death Mask of an Eighteenth-
  Century Bishop," "When We Were Children," "Pietà," "Vincent
  Van Gogh at Borinage"
Columbia: "Continuum"
Crazyhorse: "Bluefish," "Cape May"
Cutbank: "Natural History"
The Iowa Review: "Amaranth"
The Missouri Review: "Simone Weil at Le Puy"
Nantucket Review: "A Glass of Milk," "Homage to Agnes Smedley,"
  "Vines," "Rapunzel's Hair"
Ploughshares: "Psyche," "The Cruise," "Doll House"
Poetry: "The Deer," "Love Poem"
Poetry Northwest: "House," "The Land," "The Vanilla Flower,"
  "Sleeping Beauty"
Prairie Schooner: "Swallows"
The Virginia Quarterly Review: "Käthe Kollwitz," "Scar"

The author would also like to thank the New York State Council for
the Arts for a grant that aided her in the completion of this book.

FOR MY PARENTS AND FOR JIM

Contents

III

IV

The soul must learn to recognize its country in the very place of its exile.

SIMONE WEIL

I

Brides

If you call out to them
they will not hear. Once they stood at the window

after school watching the narrow path
to the house. The glass revealed its small

portion of the landscape, emptied of strangers,
buried in snow. At night their hands

sensed what they did not touch,
the body safe within its borders.

Now one by one they walk into the water,
its surface floats their gowns like masks.

Beneath the line of water and air
they are not dead but falling

as when a child falls toward its future
body, away from itself. All things drift

toward them, sway of fern, mud loosening from rock.
You think they speak but they do not.

Now it is dusk and the dresses are dredged
from the lake. And still you swim deeper and deeper

toward the shape of a woman huddled in the dark,
and although you cannot see her face

she reaches to touch you in the way of a woman
leading a child away from a grave.

The Deer

The deer is patience,
the deer is what we see standing
in the woods, half its jaw shot off,
just staring.
You ought to kill it now
but you lift it into the back of the pickup.
At home you pack the broken bone with mud.

Healing she moves toward you.
Shy, she rubs her head against your leg.
What I've loved in myself and others

is in the dream I have of this deer
though she was real: she came out of the woods
bleeding, she knew how to die
but healed. The deer that walked
one day back into the woods

is standing by a pond now, alert,
in a wash of sunlight.
How quietly she stands there
as if there were no way
to not belong in the world,
as if it were this easy.

Doll House

Chrysalis of shadows,
we kneeled before it
those long winter mornings
to learn the tender
fragility of shelter;
match-stick tables,
tiny mirrors smooth as the sea.
Our hands were giants' hands.

We learned each walled-in space
is like the heart:
small doors leading
to more doors,
long hallways giving way
to secret chambers;
the mute, expensive keys.

Like the captive flower
awaiting bloom inside the almond
light lay dormant
in ivory lamps,
flared golden
at our appointed nightfall.
Shadows drifted
fish-like through the walls.

And later, lamps
gone dark for deepest night,
the thimble-sized children
lay quiet in their beds
to feel around them
liquid walls

quivering with gills,
while far beyond them
storms enslaved
the unprotected trees.

In the deep sleep
of locked wardrobes and drawers
we buried linens, dresses,
sweet scents of lilac and rose.
This was our first grave,
all we hid and rearranged in earnest.
Its small flowers like snowflakes.
Its curtains of moonlight and dust.

Doll

Fearless, desireless,
its smooth face
impassive
as if touched by eternity,
caring nothing
for eternity.
Holding it
the child touches the pure stasis
it secretly desires
of its body,
to be as a pearl
cloistered from the world's becoming,
whole and perfect
though the universe
slowly expands,
though atoms are smashed.
The doll is a wall

with windows, eyes
open, unseeing.
Even the stars die.
But here is a world
without loss,
for see how it is empty:
inside its head, its chest,
no paths, no blossoming
flowers of blood,
no human shadows
exiled from the world
of matter,
still lingering at its edge,
held only by memory's

dim thread.
Still, the child holds it

in her sleep,
as years from now
she will hold a frozen
image of herself
inside her mind:
a child asleep within
such insufficient armor:
a wooden house
on a hill
of an ever-shifting world;
the boats unshrouded
after winter, the gray
sea rising.

Cinderella's Slipper

Longing then
was the desire
to find redemption
in forgetfulness:
ash gave way to gold
like none on earth. The horse's mane
felt smooth as silk
as it carried her past windows,
her face dissolving in each one.

Far away the cinders trembled in the hearth:
where had she gone?

At last all she saw
was far below her: patient acres,
fields spinning sunlight into crops.
White doves landed
in the oaks. They took the coarse
misshapen limbs for shelter
while she stood corsetted and gowned
above their hunger.
And the workmen stopping to rest
beside their carts,
when she waved to them
they didn't seem to see.

She dreamt of the chaste sky,
its purity was blankness.
And, gowned in silk, she dreamt
of the silkworms' lethal greed,
how they spun themselves
an endless sleep.

One day her small face
vanished from the tower.

Barefoot now, she kneels
to touch her sleeping child.
Moonseed and gentian
bow in their small plots.
The birds are strangely quiet,
inchworms nibble at the leaves.

How plain this garden is,
she thinks, and the child
who sleeps so deeply,
his blanket the only membrane
between his body and the dust;
the dust which is most faithful. . . .
See how it still veils
her skin; this ashen slipper,
this stain, this mortal love.

Natural History

Lighted, the domed roof.
Inside, in the dark,
how quiet the hallways must be,
and the animals, their heads
bowed, or they're shyly
eyeing each other.
Some drink from their

reflections, the reflected
leaves shiver out of reach.
Will they ever be released
from their bodies?
Here are the birds

that cannot fly,
and here the woodchuck
forever half-in, half-out
of the ground.
You could see their complaints
in their eyes
if their eyes were not glass.
This is their dignity.
This is how secrets

survive us somewhere else.
Six eggs in a nest,
six tight fists.
The snake that wants
to eat them but will not;
its body arched
in eternal hunger,

how safe not to get
what you want: the sky
so flat it won't
shimmer near the moon,
the pond so still
no fish will break its surface.

The Cruise

That autumn the baby died
father took us on a cruise. My sister and I
wore twin bonnets. We stuffed our fingers
into the mouths of dolls
whose eyes stared
like the sea that goes black and forever.
Nights we drifted;
the festive strung lights were a Christmas
we danced inside.
Mother's apricot skirt swirled
like petals in wind. I had seen
the ruby-throated hummingbird
fly backwards
as if into the past. . . .
But that was on land
and we did not
speak of land. We leaned
against the railing
as the coast turned to a mist;
the waves swelling, the ship
pushing them away.
I would rock myself to sleep, thinking,
there is something very beautiful in the dark
though I can't see it. One day
memory gives way to pleasure.
It's bound to happen, like the stray silver glove
that was carried by waves
to rub against the gunwale of that ship.

·

Cape May

There is a sound
a music box makes, when buried.
It is the gears
like a waterwheel embedded
in dirt, turning,

a dry-heave
of tin
making its way from the ground.

The boy lies
with his ear pressed to the sand.
Sometimes he shudders
the small cage of his voice
as he sleeps.

The beach house rests,
an unlit lantern.
Softening wood and ashen rock.
I move closer to the boy.
His body contracts.

No more than an echo
of his breath, the papery chest
rising, falling.
A leech on my nightgown,
this strand of his brown hair.

I turn from him,
fill a sack with shells,
each one a winding stair.
Against the jetty
waves break and are turned back.

Two Children

Tonight, swirl of snow
pink through the glare of high crime lights,
then slurred to gray
on city streets,
I think back to the first time
I noticed the world's diminished splendor;
myself as well, diminished, shamed.

My father's store
stood among tenements
still ripe with human life
though the outsides crumbled, were scarred.
Others were gutted:
mute skeletons that stared
in useless accusation.
Christmastime, the whole family helped out.
Children, we wore blue smock-coats,
sold buttons, cards.
Families came to buy,
but others wandered through the aisles;
loved to touch what glistened,
all they could not own.

It began with the boy
opening his fist: five pennies.
We stood beside a silvery pine,
needles bright as moonlight,
pure, unmelting snow.
The trees came in boxes,
hundreds stacked in the storeroom.
Angels that seemed to float
in a world of deafness,
you could buy one to put on top;

or the sharp tin stars
that cradled the light like water.
It began with him
putting the pennies in my hand.

It was 1963,
all the street was shining,
and I put the pennies back into his hand.
"Not enough," I said,
but couldn't make him understand.
I remember his sneakers wet with snow,
how a drunk danced through the aisles,
bottle stashed in paper bag,
toes showing through his shoes.
And still it seems we are standing in the store
though the store no longer exists.
We pass the money back and forth.
It goes on and on like this.

The Music of the Spheres

Land's end. As a child I thought these cliffs
would last forever.
But the water lulls them;

slowly they give way to its dark hungers.
And tonight, how lonely the earth seems
in its coffin of blackness;

its warmth slowly leaves it.
Unable to sleep, I think of myopic Kepler
who fashioned his image of the heavens

in a cup: each orbit cast in silver;
the moon a pearl; distant Saturn
was a diamond, crystalline perfection.

How it soothed him to hold it in his hands.
One by one his children died.
But he found comfort in the music

of the spheres, and found the Father
in the Sun: "at rest and yet the source
of motion." His bravery was this:

he treasured the music of the spheres
then proved beyond a doubt there was none.
He looked hard into the sky

and found it different from the sky
he had imagined. . . .
More than once his patience brought him

to conclusions he despised.
But what of that? It was the frankness
of the sky he loved; its sure

obsessive grace and stubborn repetitions,
how it stretched above his war-torn land,
its faithfulness undaunted.

And the sky never mourns
what it has lost: falling stars, meteors,
the snow. . . .

Seashells

Even the most ornate: amber chambers
and pearly winding stairs,
house their simple, given tenants.
Or, left empty, what remain
are soft echoes of waves, shadows
delicate as lace. Where the sky meets the sea
the sky gathers filaments of light,
sends them down in search of the intricate
Lucinas, Pandoras, where they lie hidden
in crevices and caves.
I have seen them left to bleach
in sunlight on the sand, salt-stained,
ash-gray as ancient bones. Still,
for awhile each lingers
deep, unclaimed inside the sea
where some are holding pearls:
jewels of light glistening in secret,
children carrying candles through the dark.

II

The Hazel Tree

Early summer; my young mother
reads me a story
of children lost
in the woods in winter.
Her hands turn the pages
of snow flaring blue
through bare trees. . . .

And it is years later;
I'm in the schoolyard
during recess.
My friend shows me
pictures from a book:
hollow-eyed children
knees thin
as wooden spoons,
naked women piled
behind them in a ditch.

I wander off
into a clearing.
Beneath the papery blossoms
of a hazel tree
a small woman
is weaving
a bone-white shawl.
The patient leaves
send down their shadows
to chart the lonely
rivers of her body
and sail them gently, without sound.
Her hands move back and forth

like startled birds.
Tirelessly she provides.

"I was a girl," she says,
"there was a quiet boy
who slipped a ring onto my finger
and became on one
clear summer day
a brittle constellation
in an unmarked grave."
She lowers her head,
goes back to her weaving.

I stare a long time at the ground.
When I look up again
she is gone.

The hazel tree shivers slightly in the wind.
I move closer.
White worms are eating
the white blossoms.

Continuum

In my brothers' arms I was lifted to be tossed into water,
not to die but to be saved through disappearance.

I thought I heard them calling after me,
my absence would allow them to go on.

Because I no longer need to be touched
I deny them nothing, I watch them when they sleep

and keep them safe.
Sometimes I see their faces pressed into the water's ceiling,

looking down and down as if to call me back.
Mostly I watch these walls.

Where my brothers live the houses hold their single pose,
the sky is luminous as snakeskin.

So often they find themselves walking near water—
that box planed smooth by sunlight.

Simone Weil at Le Puy

Walking to work she watches them: the unemployed;
stone cutter, coal miner,

the large idle hands she can't stop seeing
even as she steps into the schoolyard,

her girls well-scrubbed and eager,
opening their books beneath the trees.

Such a light, mathematical species,
practicing their Greek with great precision,

the sunlight come to rest on their hair
as if to insist on the ease of loveliness.

They protect their distracted teacher,
she has put her blouse on backwards!

More and more she wonders if tenderness
towards the world

eventually turns to bitterness
when you must watch the suffering of others increase,

if the mind grows dark as the mines
where coal is chipped and gathered

while those who wield it grow weak.
And yet the earth itself continues in its valor:

the hills receiving the soft light of dawn,
the grape harvest's tangled vines and swollen fruit. . . .

That night in her room she writes to a prisoner,
promises to send him some food.

Do you still miss the birds of the Pyrenees?
I don't know whether silence is not more beautiful

than all the songs!

Sleeping Beauty

A dark narrow stairway.
Each door we pass is chained
from inside; sometimes you hear the locks rattle
like the stirring of someone buried alive.

From her room you can see the lit windows,
each a golden cage
where the dark hands flutter and fall.

She wears a nightgown covered with roses.
It rests easily on her body
as if it had lain down to listen to her heart.

I don't know if her eyes see at all
as she stares at the tiled ceiling,
if she's counting the white squares.

When the man arrives she does not feel his kiss.
I want to tell her, *but that is not the story!*
you must wake up and love him!
Buses pass below the window, quietly as thieves.

The snow falling through the room is warm.
It is ashes in her hair, ashes
over her quiet face and hands.
It covers the windows, her eyes.

A Glass of Milk

How this spring field
engenders forgetfulness,
as through the locked window
I watch such endless flutterings,
deep greens beneath
the shifting light
as on the ocean
where all particulars
are hidden.
The boy beside me

rarely speaks.
The seasons are carnivorous,
he said, letting the blood
drip from his wrists
into the dead of winter.
Now most days
he walks the ward
searching for his mother's grave.
In his mind he holds

a hazel branch;
its roots would twist
into her ribcage,
she could whisper
through its leaves.
Evening, the blinds
pulled shut, he rocks
beside me.
A glass of milk
is on the table.
He will not drink it,

says poison's what
we let inside
to calm us like a lie.
I touch his bandaged wrist,
each scar a reminder
of the utter vulnerability
of the body;
and nature, fallen
through no fault
of her own,
even her mournful beauty
will not save us.
Next morning

the metal gates
swing shut behind me,
I watch the grounds recede.
Years gone, and even now
I dream I am his bride:
through sour fluorescent light
we wander dressed in white,
then lie without touching
on the ground, two lilies
for an unmarked grave.

Letter from an Institution

The azaleas are covered in black plastic.
Each week some die; a gloved hand removes them.
Where the pebbles are clustered and look like a brain
the water leaves pieces of shells.

I don't go out much anymore.
The sea is the soul of a horse kept in its stall,
its great head rocking.
I've stroked it and felt my hand grow numb.

I've learned to find the planets.
Venus is the brightest, the clouds near its surface
reflect the sun's light.
Unlike our earth it has no moon.

Once it seemed to move
and I remembered how in 1929 two aviators
flying from America to France mistook it for a beacon,
flew, they thought, straight toward that light.

The first owner of this house was a squire.
His coat of arms is burned into each door.
One spring his daughter walked out in her nightgown,
let loose his horses and dogs.

I wish I could show you how like a woman
this pine-shadow looks bending over the fence.
She would look so beautiful if she were alive.
I am so grateful she is not.

Daphne

I did not want to be touched,
now I cannot leave here.
There is a pond below the hill,
I watch my body drift there.

I thought the sky must have walls,
a ceiling I would learn to understand.
It is not so. If I could I would whisper
touch me, give me back my human form.

Nearby the old men gather in the fields,
their small fires burning under control
and the wind dying down.

Swallows

It is a kind of faithfulness, the way we wait here,
in early spring,
for the swallows—thick flurry

of russet arrows—to return.
It is our way of believing in the just and careful
turning of the seasons,

the measured, precarious world proceeding with conviction.
How beautiful the dawn is
loosening her robes.

For a moment it seems they return
because we have believed in their return,
as when belief engenders love.

The swallows tell us the earth's true names.
It is: Deeply loved but unwilling to be held.
It is: Not quite understood, Illusive shadow.

They swoop and flutter.
The trees become them, shimmering and taut.
After a long journey there is always much to do—

the branches are alive with flurry and instruction.
So little time, the swallows seem to say.
As we are their witness, and as others will be when we are gone.

The Tao of Painting

The universe was not pregnant with life, nor the biosphere with man. Our number came up in the Monte Carlo game. Is it any wonder if, like the person who just made a million at the casino, we feel strange and a little unreal?

—JACQUES MONOD

Yet the Chinese masters
would not have seen it so,
and today as I open
this book of their paintings
I recall what they believed
the world to be:
a harmony rooted in all things.
Even the trees
had their rightful place;
as here, in the east,
is the mulberry:
tree of the rising sun,
the milk of daylight
in its leaves;
and here, in the west,
grows the cassia: moonlight's
shy daughter,
its flowers mild stars
above the fields.
Nothing can destroy
such innate grace.
In the Month of the Yellow Flowers
the young men walked out
to study the blossoming
chrysanthemums,

"defiant of frost,
triumphant in autumn,"
and in painting them
paid homage
to the tenacity
of all living things.
But now, as I close the book,
I return to a world
which believes
in the fundamental
motion of all things,
as in physics the idea
of an absolute
frame of reference
is now obsolete;
and that color
is the result of the eye
responding to different
wavelengths of light.
Still, I like to think
of those young painters
surrounded by flowers,
and all around them
the blue sky
at rest above the earth.

Homage to Agnes Smedley

Night wraps the crooked branches in its cloak
as if in perpetual forgiveness. At times like this

it is possible to believe, though each embrace
occurs inside the mind and dies there, there is

a common loneliness lives on, like love,
a private yet shared world in which we recognize each other.

I felt it late last night as I watched the delicate
blue needles of the pines

bend to the wind's persistent indifference,
rough bark gone rain-soaked, rank. . . .

I fell to sleep and dreamed about that mixture
of hardship and of grace,

saw one by anonymous one
the women of the early American West

descend into a deep, communal silence,
their tired bones gone frail and white as moonlight,

eyes luminous as stars.
They showed me how the skeleton stays pure

beneath the fetid, temporal scars.
Silent, too, the men who labored their lives

for Rockefeller Fuel & Iron.
Majestic mountains surrounded such despair:

wives and daughters barefoot in calico dresses;
tiny rooms: one table, two chairs.

Sometimes I hear through the pines
the low moan of the wind

as if it carried within it all those lost voices
but I can't make out the words.

Where are the gold leaves of their suffering
that fell through the cold mountain air?

Where are their footsteps of dust?
All I have is this small tintype in my hands;

and these few pine needles
that have fallen soundlessly to earth,

softening the ground where I walk.

Rose Light through the Windows

In the eighteenth century an English duchess
designed for herself a house

made almost entirely of shells
and did not stop at dream but had it built.

For years she planned its lustrous murals
and pearly winding stairs,

skylights tinted violet and rose.
An entire house made of other houses,

that must be the point.
Not only its delicate beauty

like her own before the mirror,
but the fact that each shell, large or small,

bore the same fate
as any body: to house, to glorify,

and finally to be emptied.
How each holds to a tireless privacy

and lives in a light deflected by that privacy.
In her old age she rarely went outside

but wandered through the amber rooms,
the captive shadows

shivering like leaves;
and rocked beneath a mural of the heavens,

each star a tiny pearl.
And late at night it was as if the ocean

returned to claim it all,
the shells washed back within its realm

and she submerged in its thick darkness.
How peaceful it was then

with all the boundaries finally blurred,
the wind touching the roof as if in kindness.

The Land

Having been so long at sea she wants to touch land.
When she does it is cold, disappointing,
though from the ship it appeared a shimmering line.
In the place where desire meets remorse
the young girl lies down to sleep with such dreams
that when she wakes she appears to have aged.
She cannot explain it. How often she walks
down the street and out of someone's mind.
She does not care that they forget her.
The leaves swirling in the stream, she thinks,
they are so unlike me, bright banners
going gladly to defeat. One day among the lilacs,
the fences, the well-kept lawns
she begins to sing, "Little leaf go to sleep
in the eye of the storm
and dream a song of no one at all."

III

House

I am a keeper of secrets.
Inside me the terrible diminishments,
hands slowing to a ghostly
wavering among locked
boxes, buried treasure.
It is the women who belong to me most;
the fields will not have them.

Faithful as mirrors
these walls wait for her hands
to find them in the dark.
Even in daylight
she wanders back and forth
as if in search of something
lost: pressed flower,
pencil, silver comb.
When the man is here
her step is quicker, her voice
small as a sparrow's.

For awhile she filled me with books.
But history frightened her;
its mad in the attics,
its chains rattled in her sleep.
The sad ghosts of slaughtered
children came to her
when she was quiet;
she saw their eyes like hooks
wanting something from her.
More and more she turns
towards these chaste walls.

More and more I am sure
she will not leave me.
The clipped roses turn
towards the window
as they die; their soft mouths
close around the seeds of darkness.
She knows there are eyes
in the garden, knives
in the roadside weeds.
This morning she carried
her old clothes into the yard.
For a moment the empty dresses
filled with wind,
looked almost human as they burned.

In the Quiet House

His body, very white, what
did it feel?
And next to him a rose
until all I saw was a rose,
and the others saying
take her to her bedroom now
she's seen enough.

At night I lie down
like the snow,
sounds come to my window
but I send them away.

His quiet room. On the other
side of the wall he turned
in his sleep, coughed
like the sound of paper tearing.
Daytimes propped up
in his wheelchair
he watched while I played.
I made for him a necklace
of white clover,
stars
he could be sky to.
I looked for worms
glistening like rainbows
in the street.
It seemed they'd live forever,
that growing smaller
didn't hurt their hearts.
And then came winter.

The dolls on the shelf
stare into my eyes
and stare into my eyes.
Outside the window
there is more land than I can imagine
and no one is out walking.

When We Were Children

attics were strong fortresses,
or, with beamed ceilings and walls
like the weather-beaten, oil-stained hull of a ship
they sailed us
past the rooftops, into clouds.
How comforting that was

as it was comforting to see, last night, at sunset,
two chestnut horses
keeping a calm gait along the shore.
The red sun was setting in their backs
and seemed to guide them onwards. They went so quietly

as if compelled by a diligent privacy,
complete and everlasting.
I thought of the waves
behind them:
once set in motion
they couldn't help but to keep breaking
with great fanfare,
whereas the self, I think,
possesses a great reticence,
not unlike the white camellias
opening slowly after storm.
Sister, that first time

death came into our house
and spread her shawls, her delicate
confusing webs of lace,
we climbed into the attic,
tried on ancient clothes.
Such whispers then of crinolines and silks!

Such purple feathers waiting in the dust!
Moths had eaten

not half so much as they had left.
In amber light, the frosted windows
blocking out what sunlight
would reveal: brick houses,
the chimneys' fading wisps of smoke,
we placed our feet into silk stockings.
You kneeled before me on the dusty floor.
For a moment dying seemed a gentle thing:

She drew her foot out of the heavy wooden shoe
and placed it in the shining slipper
which fitted like a glove.

Pietà

Mother and son.
A quiet surrounds them
as if it were rising
from their bodies.
The mother alive,
the son now dead
resting in her lap
as if he could dissolve there.

One of her hands
touches the very tips
of his fingers
that, having suffered,
have resolved
into a stillness
beyond her understanding.

There is no end
to this embrace
though the woman will rise
to falteringly resume
her daily chores,
obedient to the air
still gently entering her body,
making breath as easily
as once she made milk.

But for now
her mind wanders;
she pictures the gulls
she watched long ago:
in them obedience

and will were
indistinguishable,
they'd drift as the air drifts,
rising and falling,
their wings barely moving.

Now, for her, the world
is a fragile and beautiful flame
swaying in wind,
slowly fading
like a distant star
dissolving, voiceless,
into dawn.

The Vanilla Flower

The pale yellow-green vanilla flower
opens for one day of its lifetime; too rapidly the light

withdraws into evening, tossing its keys into the river.
There are losses we won't admit to

except in dreams—the petals spreading in silence,
the air touching so briefly the soft inner skin.

Maybe this evening a woman walks out onto a lawn
where everyone is dancing.

A man approaches and they too begin to dance.
They have not yet been cruel to one another.

They swirl until the sun is an orchid and the wind
seems to be sighing

though they both think this strange
since neither feels enough desire to be sad,

just as the vanilla flower so cool in the night
is wrapped in the dream of its own taut skin.

How tightly a body curls
when the mind dreams of leaving,

knowing that to journey is to lose the light
returning always to one place,

and the shadows soothing the toppled barn,
laying their scarves gently down.

Remember how someone you loved turned sorrowfully away.
It is deep into night

and the vanilla flower, shy, wanting safety,
has shut severely,

though its vine climbs to the highest tree tops
and the leathery leaves fare well in harsh weather.

Spider Web

Towards summer's end
I found it
strung between two trees,
ghost-ship trembling
in slightest wind.
Even at night it shimmered,
made visible by moonlight
pale and detached
above the bay.
An overhang of roof
kept it sheltered.

My neighbors
boarded up their house
and still it stayed,
jeweled with the small
cold bodies of their garden,
wasp wings stiffened
to delicate fans,
the husks of black flies.

The thick leaves
reddened and fell.
Still it remained.
The plump berries
shriveled on their vines,
and it remained:
breath-misted looking-glass
holding within it
the white branches of winter,
slumber and frost,
promise and decay.

When the spider died
it still held
the delicate eggs,
quiet, fist-tight;
how they slept within
such patience:
House without rooftop
or beams; no doors
but the intricate locks
grasping, unfastening.
The tranquil light
inside the storm.
Fingerprint and star.

Käthe Kollwitz

This morning, sketching in the garden,
suddenly it occurred to me:
I do not think of these flowers
as lovely. Their bright colors
hurt my mind, for they are crimson
as blood seeping from a wounded son,
purple as the bruise on the forehead
of the awkward boy who waited in my doorway
to tell me how his comrade died.
I tell it to myself again
as if to test its truth: my son grew up
to die a soldier. I draw his face
anonymous, gray. Gray mist and rain.
Gray stone. At night I dream I give the children
smiling dolls to hold before they sleep.
Now, while they lie alone, untouched,
warm in little cribs. Now,
while there's still joy, like a falling star,
inside their bodies.

Lost

Like a girl laying wreathes
on the water, clouds darken
the edges of the river.
Leaves flutter pale as hands.
In the rubble a brown mare,
scorched and eyeless,
searches for its stable,
turns in circles in the street,
pure elegance defiled
by despair. Its long skull
caked with blood
swings to the left,
to the right, as if listening
for its master's voice
or the simple sound of a bird
rustling its feathers in a tree.
Exhausted, it lies down
beside a girl whose face is swollen
black with burns;
their mixed blood
stains the ashen earth.
Her hands against her eyes
she dreams that all the chrysanthemums
bloom at once before they die;
the whole landscape for an instant
a sea of white blossoms,
some to be woven
into the long braids of a bride,
some for her satin pillow.

Psyche

There is a face—
smooth, hard,
a knot of polished wood.
Each night it burns in my hands.

Wood is smooth and has no breath.
Tap it again and again.
It sounds like someone approaching.

He lies at the bottom of a lake,
I float above.
Unable to lift him to this surface,
unable to make myself drown,
I watch the dark line of his body.

Fingernails on wood:
music heard through the sweep of a broom,
something scratching the door.

As a child, I curled at my mother's
side in the bed. I believed I touched
my future body, her breathing carried me
forward like cradled arms.

Wood underneath the body's full weight
will not give.
Pressed to the palm of a hand
it resembles that hand.

I place a lamp at the bedside.
Its shadow on the wall: an hourglass,

a cage. When he enters this room
I will know every line of his face,
I will lose him. Light sifts
through the air like ash.

Vines

It is as if they knew
about the world, the slow dissolution
of objects, that they cling so
to wall or stem; as if

through such tenacity
they could keep the present
from falling away,
and make the earth eternal:

the woman thinks this
as she stands on a glass-enclosed
balcony in the city.
She remembers the night
she looked out on a world
blurred by storm;
how she imagined herself
at the edge of a pond
in which the dead were rooted.
There was no sorrow
in their bondage, they turned
toward each other
as toward the sun.
They perceived no horizon line
and were content.
They did not think of the astronaut
torn from his orbit,
drifting deeper
and deeper into space.
They did not worry
about loss of direction,
how the living are never

without roads.
But she remembers

something else as well;
how that night
as she stood on the balcony,
a bird, not revery or wish,
rose up out of the storm,
hurled itself again and again
against the glass,
its head softening
until finally it fell;

and her hands tightened
like vines around
the objects in her pockets,
as if through pure insistence
she could have stopped
the bird from falling;
and the storm moved on, numb
above the small, tortured body.

Death Mask of an Eighteenth-Century Bishop

Like history, its surface
is fixed, a pond closing over stones.
The thin mouth looks troubled
though it's impossible to know for sure.
I imagine the eyes to be kind,
to suffer bravely the dark
which is endless and full of loss.
Here the doubleness of self survives:
one face softening among the spidery roots,
the other displayed under glass
where the living penetrate their own reflections
to witness this slave to endless silence;
how that which came before us
claims us still.
How pure and yet past innocence.
At night in the empty room
it shines white as stars.

Snowfall

This deafness of the earth once again inside its shell.
We can't forget what we were born for:
How we long to be covered with water as if sleeping with water.
The little ones lie down in the swollen fields.

IV

Electra, Waiting

This is the solace of the soil: wet with slaughter
it still knows no tyranny nor treason;

the smallest flower
finds its place between the rocks,

the shallow-rooted cactus hoards water in its stem,
it lives on what is hidden.

Each night through my window I see how the moon
loves the earth from a great distance,

never drawing near.
Some nights she hides most of her face.

I hide in the smallest chamber of the palace.
I have heard of a tree

which blossoms only once each hundred years.
It keeps its deepest nature

secret; many must believe it barren.
How patient the earth is!—its winter trees,

its mountains diminishing more slowly than can be seen.
Each year I cut my hair

and place it on my father's grave.
The bitter tree which grows there

sways gently in the wind; I rest my hands
between its branches as if between his hands.

Nights I serve his enemies their food.
But each day that tree grows stronger,

its leaves like vultures casting shadows on the land,
vigilant as prophecy, more faithful than kind.

Rapunzel's Hair

Evening light
feathering the grass,
that's what it was,
when in the soft meadows
the flowers became
again locked rooms,
and the whole landscape
as well (wide doors
of shadows on the hillsides)
seemed a closing up.
Only then
would her golden hair
fall free
from the tower;
not like starlight
which mirrors
pure desire,
but yellow leaves
breaking free
from their branches
and tumbling to earth;
the transformation
of desire into love.
And how like a road
of dust it was,
a secret pathway
leading out
of a plundered town
where children huddled
at hearthside, later
knelt beside their beds,
eyes raised toward the far

unanswering dark.
Still, how like a rope
it was, a silken ladder
one might climb
not toward perfection
or the embodiment
of faith,
but up the side
of a bare, stairless tower
with one small window
through which to enter,
and inside, a stark,
quiet room, where
for awhile one might rest.

Swamp Blackberry

Over soft, wet earth
it crawls
as if in search
of shelter,
though even the supplest ground
keeps it out.
There is no way
to escape
being brave; it journeys
onward, tangled
in itself, stretching
farther and farther
away from its roots.
Early summer, each green calyx,
a modest armor,
folds back
in order that the five
white petals
it has sheltered
emerge to hold
their smallest cup of light.
Such tender fists
unfolding. And, once opened,
how finely gowned
they are, like brides,
sheltered by rooftops
of green leaves,
thorned fences
of red stems.
Here they will outgrow
their white reluctance,
thick with bees

before they fall;
each blossom
mortal and replaceable
though infinitely
lovely in itself.
And when they're gone
the birds still sing.
And when they're gone
the light remains.

Staying Home from Work

Thousands of crystals, small luminous windows,
snowflakes fall
like the myriad and insufficient
explanations of a life,

though as they touch ground
they seem to become something else—
a soft blanket of moonlight
covering the earth as it dreams.

How warm my house is!
And the tea steeping in its cup between my hands.
I stay inside all afternoon and read a tale
of an old scholar

who spends his afternoons
in the wineshops of Lo Ching.
The townspeople laugh at his "gibberish,"
laugh because he steals

books instead of food.
And they are most filled with mirth
on the day that he crawls on his stomach,
pulling himself forward by his arms

into the wineshop,
because his legs have been broken
as punishment for stealing.
He drinks in silence;

his hands caked with mud
warm around his bowl of wine.

He says nothing when he leaves
and is never seen again.

I finish my tea
that is warm and smells of lemons.
I close my eyes and know that the snow
is still falling

like all the words he didn't say,
that it is covering the hushed and troubled earth
like a wonderful secret,
like a door not meant to be opened.

Scar

The ferry moves from shore
towards the islands, quiet as sleepers.

How far away the tall buildings seem
and the old men rummaging through trash cans.

But when I fall off to sleep
I still dream of the knife

the rapist held beneath my eye,
how part of my mind ticked abstractly on:

the knife, it is beautiful, a flame
that will not die.

The ferry moves forward through the night,
the pale moon slowly eclipsed by the clouds.

I had a friend who lost most of his face
before he died, the cancer like ants

eating him alive. He wore gauze
to cover up the scars so strangers

wouldn't flinch. One Sunday we went fishing.
I looked into his eyes and was afraid.

Together we rocked in our little boat.
Sometimes I touch the scar beneath my eye

as if I could reach down inside it
to find the rapist's face

still sneering, talking to itself,
wet and soft as a fetus.

Sometimes I stare into a fireplace
and see in the ashen, crumbling wood

my friend's ruined face.
The ferry bears its few lights

towards the islands, through what appears
to be emptiness, without end.

Bluefish

Opened by the knife
it is beautiful
archeology,
abstract as desires
the body has abandoned.

Its eyes a milky blue.
Its scales prisms
that break light.
Its whole body arched
toward death
the way a woman
having placed a stone
in each pocket
enters the still water.

We wrap it in plastic,
take it to the car.
But once beneath sunlight
and a knife,
its body, opened,
was strangely undiminished.
Intricate cage.

Beasts of Burden

They rise up silently
out of the mists of early morning. What blossoms

blossoms beyond them; bees deep in tender petals,
the proud, erratic flutterings of birds.

Having known the persistence of force
they have grown deeply quiet, as a leaf is quiet,

or a stone. And as they bow
beneath the weight of what they carry

they do not think to cast it off,
it is to them the world—frayed rope, rough cloth,

the burlap sacks that urge them downward
towards the soft, submissive earth.

They have learned their lessons well;
they do not even try to rest

against the grass that breathes like sleep.
Nor do they tremble

when the whip bears down against their bones.
Fear was long ago. Now, in their gentleness,

they are most alone.
Their tired bones are secret pathways

dissolving into darkness, the stillness of an autumn field.
Their hunger is a field inside them

where each night the moon comes down
through twisted branches

to give itself completely
to the tranquil water pooled beneath the leaves.

Vincent Van Gogh at Borinage

Because the land is always changing
it is beautiful. The secretive black earth

gives way, in time, to fullness: green corn,
the five white petals of the blackberry flower

opening in unison, fluttering like moths.
And now the earth, asleep beneath the snow,

needs rest in order to go on.
Beneath the ground are cells: the miners

laboring where light can't reach.
There is still so much slavery in the world,

he thinks, pausing to warm his hands by the fire,
then watching through his window

as a white horse walks slowly
down the frozen road; it pulls a cart

in which a wounded miner lies,
turning his face from the sun.

Each twilight the miners, black figures
over the snow, head back towards town,

lines of them emerging from the earth,
a chain across the land.

The yellow light in his window flickers as they pass.
They do not notice that he draws them

or know how in his dreams he sees their faces
beautifully injured and worn as barren branches

in a season of abundance.
He walks at night among the mounds of coal

as if searching for a child's tiny grave,
and kneels beside the shafts

precarious as bone,
the blackened wagons waiting to be filled.

Love Poem

After the flesh is stripped and cut for meat
the whale's skull is launched into water, an empty cage

the ocean moves through, a house consumed by fire.
The white skull floats out

as if it could grow flesh again, surface
in the Arctic, the sound of its breath preceding it

by miles. Boats trace that sound
to where the whales rise, volcanic, webbed in kelp.

Sunlight is a shroud. The whale and boat draw closer.

The Stone House

My husband's body
softens in the sea.
Nights he would not touch me
but described the rooms
that would be mine
when he was dead.
I never dreamed I'd kill him.
His white hair pooled
like moonlight on my wrists.

Twenty rooms there are
within this house.
Each, he said, more lovely
than the next.
One day when he was out
I turned the keys
inside their slippery locks,
I turned the key
I promised not to turn.
At first I only saw
the starkness of those
crumbling walls,
empty clothes like unstrung
puppets on the floor.

Now each night I walk again
into that bloody room.
The pieces of the children
start to reassemble.
Like trees they sway.
Their arms are slender branches;
blood falls from them like leaves.

I press my lips against their lips
until they breathe.

By morning they are dead again.
I hear my husband struggling back
against the waves.

Beneath the ruinous
gold leaves of autumn
I walk to where the sea
rises, a withered hand,
against the cliffs. Far off,
white sails glide by like swans.
I wonder vaguely if they see me.
And still I hear the children
weeping in their jagged sleep.
The sun begins to set.
I head for home. Stars
stir like embers
in the quiet sky.

Amaranth

Imagine it,
the Amaranth is said to be undying,
its petals like pearls
harboring the pink light
of sunsets.
It is forgiveness.
It is the peasant who refuses
to abdicate
his small patch of land.
Someone sad
must have invented it,
perhaps as he watched
thick flocks of sparrows
fleeing from winter,
and felt the hands of famine
cradling his home.
So he imagined its leaves
tender as butterflies
and its stubborn center
domestic as hairpins.
In wind, it would rustle
like pages of a book
treasured since childhood,
"Far off and long ago,"
it might begin, and end,
"Although the oldest daughter
died as a child
in a cold, dark tower,
the others had many children
and lived for a long time
through many seasons
and through many
changes of heart."

Other Titles in the Contemporary Poetry Series